Reading Time

CW01639021

The Hound of the Baskervilles

Juliette Saumande
d'après l'œuvre de Sir Arthur Conan Doyle

Illustré par **Benoît Perroud**

Relu et commenté par **Claire Béniméli**, professeur certifiée d'anglais, anciennement formatrice en IUFM

hachette
ÉDUCATION

My name is Doctor Watson. You probably don't know me. But I'm sure you know my friend, Sherlock Holmes. He is the best private detective in England.

"My dear Watson" he said one day, "this is Sir Henry Baskerville. He has a mystery for us. Let's hear it!"

"I come from Devonshire" Sir Henry said. "In our village, there is a legend about a giant dog. We call it 'the Hound of the Baskervilles' because this dog only attacks members of the Baskerville family. People think this dog is supernatural and they are all terrified."

"What a strange story!" I said.

"I know" Sir Henry said. "But last June, my uncle, Sir Charles Baskerville, died."

"How did he die?" asked Holmes.

"He was in the garden*, at night. He was old and ill. He probably had a heart attack."

Sherlock Holmes smoked his pipe.
"What is the mystery, Sir Henry?" he asked.
"Near my uncle's body," he said "I saw the giant footprints* of an enormous dog! But it can't be the Hound of the Baskervilles: it's only a legend, isn't it?"
"We will see..." Holmes promised.

So, the next day, I went to Devonshire with Sir Henry. Holmes stayed in London to finish work. There were a lot of soldiers* in the little village. "We are searching for Selden, the dangerous criminal" a soldier said. "He escaped from prison."

Finally, we arrived at Baskerville Hall.
"This is Mr Barrymore and his wife" Sir Henry said. "They are my servants."
Mr and Mrs Barrymore were strange. They were very polite, but Mrs Barrymore's eyes were red.
*Did she cry**? I asked myself.
What is her secret?

The next day, I saw Mr and Miss Stapleton, the neighbours. Mr Stapleton was a naturalist. He loved to study insects and plants. He lived with his sister in the middle of the countryside.
"What a strange place!" I said. "No trees*, just grass* and rocks*."
"We call it the moor" Mr Stapleton explained. "It is very dangerous. Don't fall in the mud* or you will disappear forever."

After lunch, I discovered a note in my pocket*.
Tell Sir Henry to go away! Or he will die! Miss S.

That night, there was a noise outside my bedroom.
"Who is here?" I asked. No answer.

In the corridor, I saw Mr Barrymore.
He was walking silently with a candle* in his hand.
He went to a window* and opened it.
"What are you doing?" I asked.

Barrymore was really surprised. And he was terrified.
"I'm sending a signal" he explained. "It says: *there is food in the garden*."
"Why?"
"It's for Selden, the criminal" he said quietly.
"He is my wife's brother and he is hungry. I'm sorry."
So that was the Barrymores' secret.

I called Sir Henry and we ran outside.
It was very dark.
"Look!" I said. "Selden! I see his white shirt*!"
We ran and ran. But Selden was fast. Finally, he disappeared.
"Let's go home!" Sir Henry said. "I'm tired*."
But at that moment, there was a terrible sound:
booooow boowwww!
"It's the dog!" Sir Henry said. "The Hound of the Baskervilles!"

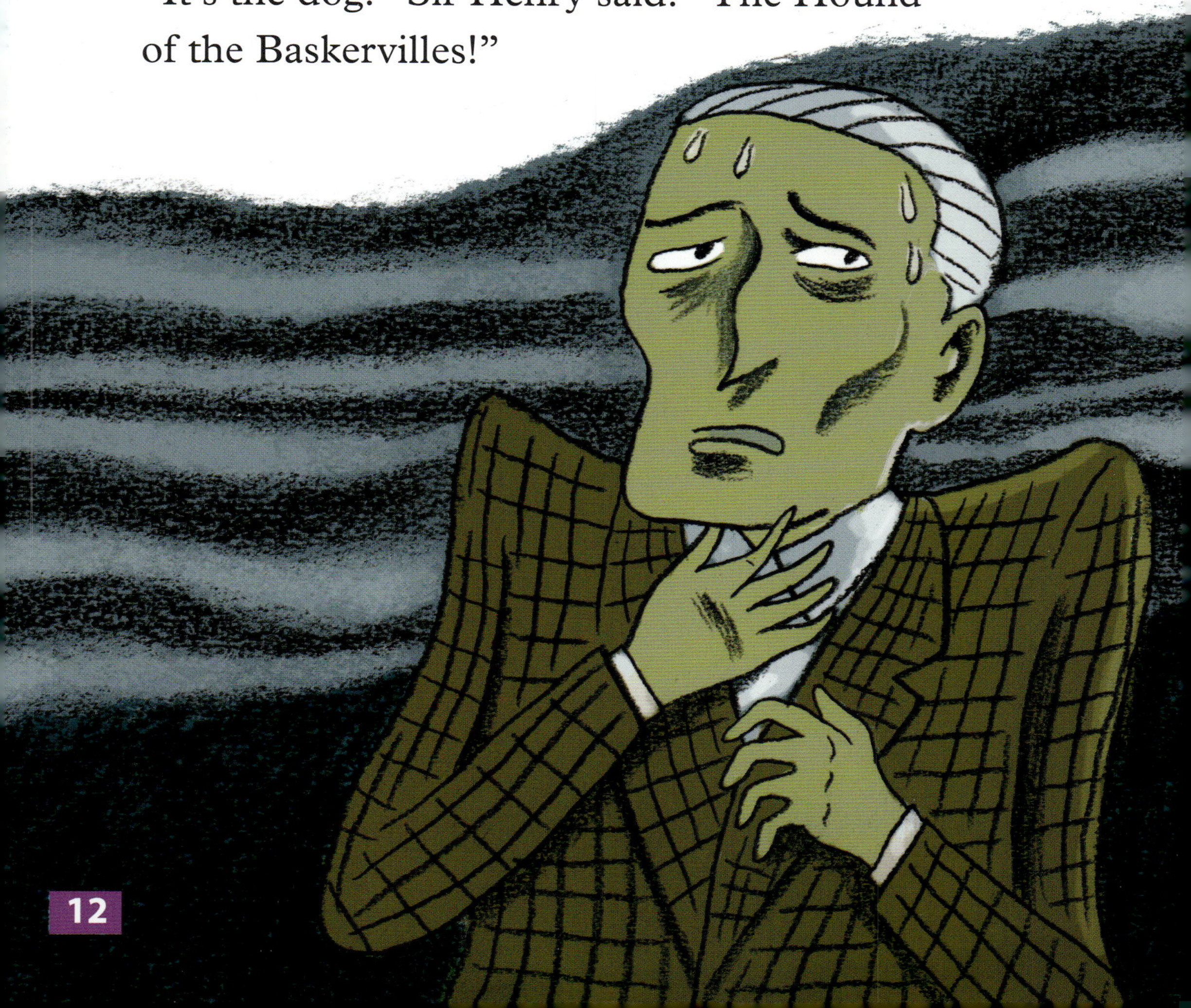

We waited. The sound stopped. Suddenly, the moon* appeared.

"There!" I exclaimed. "On the rocks! A man! And it's not Selden!"

I ran again, but I was too late.

The next morning, I went for a walk on the moor.
But soon, I was lost.
*A farmer's hut**! *I will ask for help.*
The door was open, but the hut was empty.
The table was full of old newspapers*.
I looked at them: *Sir Charles Baskerville dies mysteriously. Who killed Sir Charles Baskerville?*

Who lives here? I asked myself.
Is it the murderer? Let's wait for him!

Finally, there was a noise outside.
I armed my pistol. The door opened slowly.
A man appeared. "My dear Watson" he said.
"How are you?" It was Sherlock Holmes!

"I am here *incognito*" Holmes explained.
"I am observing all the houses and the people near Baskerville Hall, day and night."
"The man on the rocks!" I realised. "Was it you?"
"It was. Now, what's the news? Tell me."
I obeyed. But suddenly…

Boooow boowwww!

That horrible sound again!

We ran outside. Soon, Holmes stopped.

"Look!" he said.

There was a man on the ground, with a lot of blood* on his face. It was Selden and he was dead.

"And here!" Holmes said. "Giant dog footprints!"

The Hound of the Baskervilles!

THE SOLUTION

At Baskerville Hall, we called the police.
The phone was in the painting gallery.
"What a great collection of family portraits!"
Holmes exclaimed. "Now I know who killed
Sir Charles! Look at this ancestor.
His face is familiar, isn't it?"

"Yes!" I said. "Mr Stapleton resembles him!"
"I think" Holmes continued "that Mr Stapleton is a Baskerville too. He wanted to inherit the family's money, so he killed Sir Charles."
"How?"
"He frightened him with a big dog and the old man had a heart attack" Holmes explained.
"But I'm going to arrest him. Here's my plan..."

The next day, after dinner with the Stapletons, Sir Henry walked back to Baskerville Hall. Holmes and I waited on the rocks near the road*. Suddenly, there was that terrible sound again and we saw the dog. It was enormous, but it was real.
"And here's Mr Stapleton!" I said.
"Quick, Watson!"

I armed my pistol and *bang*! I killed the dog. Mr Stapleton ran on the moor. But he fell into a lake of mud. He slowly disappeared.
The murderer and his dog were dead.
That was the end of the legend of the Hound of the Baskervilles.

Lexicon

a garden

a footprint

a soldier

to cry

a tree

grass

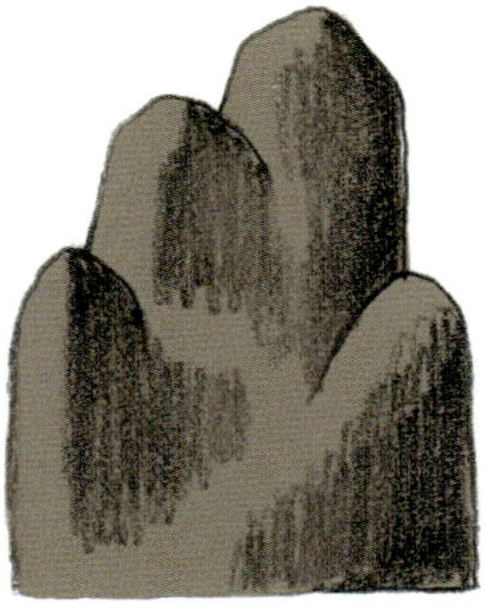

a rock

the mud

a pocket

a candle

a window

a shirt

tired

the moon

a hut

a newspaper

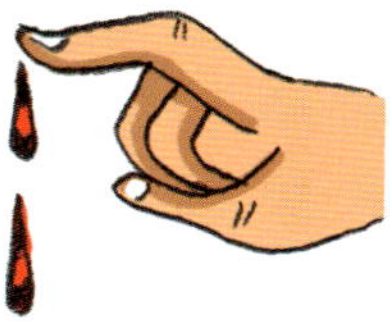

blood

a road

Contents

PAPIER À BASE DE FIBRES CERTIFIÉES

hachette s'engage pour l'environnement en réduisant l'empreinte carbone de ses livres. Celle de cet exemplaire est de :
300 g éq. CO_2
Rendez-vous sur www.hachette-durable.fr

Responsable de projet : Marie Lucas
Conception graphique et mise en page : Estelle Chandelier

ISBN : 978-2-01-117545-8
© Hachette Livre 2015, 58, rue Jean Bleuzen, CS 70007, 92178 Vanves cedex.
Tous droits de traduction, de reproduction et d'adaptation réservés pour tous pays.

Imprimé en France par Imprimerie CHIRAT - 42540 Saint-Just-la-Pendue - N° 202107.0226
Dépôt légal : Août 2021 - Collection n° 69 - Édition 06 - 11/7545/4